BUDDIES

Men. Dogs. And World War II.

Dedication

This book is dedicated to the war correspondents of World War II. Even in the darkest days of the battles, the clever captions and playful photographs by these unkown journalists helped our nation hold out hope—and sometimes, even smile.

BUDDIES

Men. Dogs. And World War II.

L. Douglas Keeney

First published in 2001 by MBI Publishing Company, 729
Prospect Avenue, PO Box 1, Osceola, WI 54020-0001 USA

MBI Publishing Company books are also available at
discounts in bulk quantity for industrial or sales-promotional
use. For details write to Special Sales Manager at Motorbooks
International Wholesalers & Distributors, 729 Prospect
Avenue, PO Box 1, Osceola, WI 54020-0001 USA.

Library of Congress Cataloging-in-Publication Data Available
ISBN 0-7603-1020-3

On the cover: Saki, a black cocker mascot is shown with one
of his pals, Seaman First Class Kenneth Smith of Clawson,
Michigan. Saki appears on page 93.

On the titlepage: Kelly, a mascot aboard an invasion
transport ship in the Far Pacific, appears on page 95.

Edited by John Adams-Graf
Designed by Dan Perry

Printed in China

Contents

Foreword   6

Introduction   7

Chapter 1   Dogs and Dogfaces: Mascots of the Army   17

Chapter 2   Dog Fights: Mascots of the Army Air Forces   31

Chapter 3   Salty Dogs: Dogs of the U.S. Navy   53

Chapter 4   Dog Tags: Mascots of the U.S. Coast Guard   73

Chapter 5   Semper Fido: The Mascots of the U.S. Marine Corps   121

Chapter 6   Jubilee: War's End   137

Chapter 7   Who Said I'm a Dog? Humor in the Face of War   143

Index   156

Foreword

This book came about quite by accident. While researching World War II photography at the National Archives for a book about the air war over Nazi Europe, I came across a small collection of mascot photos. The photos reposed in a record group that hadn't been much in circulation, and that alone was exciting enough, but what intrigued me most was that the dogs portrayed were mutts. These weren't the well-bred dogs of West Point or the Naval Academy or anything like that—these were just average animals adopted in the field by the average kind of guy sent over to fight the war.

I looked at my unexpected discovery and something caught my eye. Perhaps it was the composition, or maybe it was the writing, but something told me that these photographs were just the tip of an iceberg. Little did I know how massive this berg would be.

Developing this collection has been one of the most difficult, time-consuming tasks in my many years as an author. Finding what one wants in the photographic archives of World War II is not an easy thing. It invariably means one must research through the holdings the old-fashioned way—with fingers passing through box after box after box of original combat prints. Tens of thousands of prints passed before my eyes, if not many, many more.

I owe several debts of gratitude. First of all, to Kate Flaherty, a research assistant at the National Archives, who was familiar with dog photography and who helped me sift through the individual collections from each of the branches. Many times she steered my hands toward richer veins of material. Also to Mark Forman, my digital assistant and art director, who went to Washington to help digitize these images. I must also thank my editor, John Adams-Graf, whose many suggestions helped shape this material, and to Zack Miller, my publisher, who steered the project through the corridors at MBI Publishing Company in Osceola, Wisconsin. Finally, to my wife, Jill Johnson Keeney, and my two sons, Dougo and Alex, who complained little despite my many days away on this project. It may have started by accident, but that this book came about at all is a tribute to the many people who helped me see it through.

Introduction

On December 3, 1942, the public affairs office at the Army base at Fort Benning, Georgia, put out a rather unusual press release. Among the notable oddities about it was this: It was three pages long. Considering the times, what news was important enough to justify three pages? On every front, World War II was going very poorly indeed. In Europe, Army Air Forces B-17s and B-24s were being brutally decimated by battle-hardened German fighter pilots while, in the Pacific, the land and sea battles on Guadalcanal were swinging back and forth with no clear victor in sight.

In its own way, it was just as bad on the home front. Life was austere, Spartan, and governed almost entirely by the dictates of necessity and scarcity. The tempo of everyday existence moved to the incessant drumbeat of bond drives and the urgent need to gather up scraps of metal and aluminum and leather and whatever else could be quickly turned into bullets, canteens, and shoes for our soldiers. "Bang! Bang!" went the drum, and why not? Who could rest when America's sons were in such great peril and needed so much? As one of the thousands of war posters said, "*Keep Moving. Don't Waste a Precious Minute.*"

Yet Fort Benning sent three pages of news into these hurried times. What could be so important? As it happened, it was a story about a "nine-pound, rust-colored boxer named Max" who had just

Building TBM seaplanes in Baltimore. As an entire nation rushed to war, simple delights like mascot photography helped men endure the pressures and fear of combat.

completed the requisite jumps to earn the most coveted of all Army honors, his parachute wings.

What made this story unusual was this: Max was a dog.

Within a year of Pearl Harbor, America was entrenched in war. The need to feed, clothe, and equip millions of our soldiers forced the vast majority of our factories to run overtime. Shoe manufacturers turned out combat boots. K rations rolled down the food processors. Automobile plants switched to making jeeps, tanks, bombers, and fighters. On both coasts and on the Gulf of Mexico, boat yards hummed with activity throughout the day and then sparkled at night with the hiss and pop of welding arcs.

But it wasn't just the manufacturing sector that was hard at work. In times of war one has to win the hearts and souls of the home front, too, and so the communications arts went to war as well. Writers, designers, actors, photographers, illustrators, and every manner of communication specialist went to work. Hollywood luminaries such as John Ford, John Houston, Frank Capra, and William Wyler enlisted themselves to the task of producing newsreels, training films, and documentaries, many of which went on to win Academy Awards.

Cartoonists went to war as well. Animated short-subject films using a character called Private Snafu proliferated. Private Snafu's mischief

B-26 Marauder pilot. This was the flesh and blood of World War II—the boys from back home.

taught the farm-boys-turned-soldiers the burden of responsibility in the military, delving into some touchy issues like morality, dating in foreign cities, conscientiousness, and other strikingly forthright topics.

But what of the fourth estate—the press corps? Despite my years of studying and writing about World War II, I knew of no body of work that distinctly represented the war output of the war correspondents of the U.S. military, and this brought me back to the three-page press release about the dog named Max. Max's release was too good to have been a one-shot thing. It was well written, poised, and well thought out; it was skillfully photographed, too. But should that have been a surprise? Many of the war correspondents had been brilliant publicists in their civilian lives. Just because no one had collected their work didn't mean they hadn't done some rather extraordinary things. Was dog photography their poster art, their Private Snafu, their award-winning documentary productions? Was this an over-looked contribution? Judging from the professionalism of the Max piece, I was willing to bet that it was.

Marine Corps war correspondents, 1943. For a nation hungry for news about its boys, a willing corps of correspondents created a genre of photography that reassured the home front that, yes, their boys were still boys.

I decided to go to Washington, D.C., and do some research. I quickly found that I was on the right track. In 1994, a junior curator within the Still Media Records section of the National Archives in College Park, Maryland, had likewise sensed that a body of World War II work had yet to be catalogued and had herself researched their holdings sufficient to assemble a small collection of soldiers and animals. The photography was striking and forthright, but her work, as a whole, fell short of the mark. Funds were cut back and her collection only skimmed the surface of the subject matter. She had scarcely more than 30 photographs and her theme was blurred, covering all types of animals seen during the war, many of those the horses and mules enlisted to carry supplies, but not necessarily mascots, and with no emphasis on the home front at all.

An earlier curator, in the early 1950s, had fared better in the World War II records of the U.S. Coast Guard. Although the name of this researcher has long been lost to history, this person got to the heart of the matter. Two, well-worn boxes tightly packed with over 100 aged photographs like Max's had been left behind for future generations to discover. They were magnificent photographs: poignant, artful, and inspired. All of the captions were carefully thought out and written to reassure loved ones back home that their boys were all right. I could only imagine the hundreds of hours this person spent culling through the records of the U.S. Coast Guard to separate out this marvelous collection. Many of the examples found by this now-anonymous researcher appear in the appropriate section of this book.

Giddy over my good fortune in the Coast Guard records, I eagerly turned to the other files, but there my luck ended. Sadly, that nameless researcher had only worked the relatively small collection of the Coast Guard files. Now the going would truly get tough. Ahead of me lay the largest record groups in the building—1,200,000 images from the Army, approximately 750,000 images from the Navy, over 500,000 from the Army Air Force, and another 52,164 from the Marines. So, over the course of two years, I went back and forth to Washington, delving deeper into the files. I wrote up countless pull slips and requested hundreds of boxes of archival photos, each crammed with original World War II combat prints, some bulging with almost 1,000 images each.

Photo by photo, I found individual treasures in the Navy, Air Force, Marine Corps, and Signal Corps archives. Most of the mascot photographs also surfaced one by one, while some emerged in small runs of 5 or 10 images. There they were the unmistakable handiwork of the war correspondents, the signature product of the fourth estate: soldiers and their dogs, photographed for the home front, set to captions that were sure to make even the most despondent mother smile. My files grew from 100 images to 200, then to 400 and more, all of similar artistic style, all captioned in a playful voice, all showing a homeboy soldier, and his mascot. And all of them sent to the local newspapers back home.

In truth, mascot photography, dog photography, buddy photography—whatever you want to call it—proliferated during World War II. It began with a scattering of shots in the early months of the war, but as the build-up accelerated and casualties mounted, war correspondents began to make this material a routine, predictable element included in their dispatch photography sent back home. Mascots were woven into the fabric of a soldier's World War II life and when one played with his pet, out came a camera. As a result, a genre emerged. Photos of "buddies"—soldiers and their dogs—conveyed to the people on the home front that their boys, in spite of the horrors they faced, were still boys. A B-17 crew, though normally ferrying tons of bombs to unload on targets deep into Germany, found the time to rig an oxygen mask for its dog. Almost without question, this glimmer of playfulness was photographed. When it became known that a reconnaissance squadron in England had a pet bear, a photographer rushed out to snap a record of the crew and their pet. Something as simple as a GI stuffing a stowaway dog into his duffel bag caught the attention of the lens, and in turn, that of a concerned nation, anxiously awaiting any news from their boys. The soldier and his dog seemed to be a theme worth repeating. The images conveyed innocence, simplicity, and gentleness in the face of something so horrific.

Wherever they were, mascots were photographed and captioned, and the images were quickly placed on a flight back to the United States. The photographs alone are endearing but, like slogans printed on poster art, much of the good-feel of a mascot picture came from its caption. Captioning became an art. It was a chance for the war correspondents to go beyond the bonds of everyday journalism and exercise their God-given abilities to creatively write, and some rather considerable talents were poured into these short paragraphs. These imaginative correspondents added whimsical stories and light-hearted prose to their poignant photos. Some even added story and plot. "Sinbad, the famous mascot of a Coast Guard combat cutter, is in the doghouse again," begins one caption. "After a big night of shore liberty with the boys, he failed to muster and stayed in the sack, in his specially made sea hammock. Sinbad is a gay blade with the ladies and, surpassing his shipmates, has several in every port." Says another: "Kelly is the salty mascot of an invasion transport now helping to kick the daylights out of the Japs in the Far Pacific. He's down on the ship's roster as a gunner's mate second class, promoted two jumps for his exceptional barking at Saipan."

How irresistible this is, even to this day—just imagine how uplifting it must have been then: an innocent dog and one of the boys, himself an innocent as vulnerable as his mascot, transformed and relaxed in the midst of war. In their day, editors clearly agreed that this new genre worked: One such photograph won a National Press Club Award (see the sad dog on page 93). Others made it into the branch magazines like *Impact*, *Air Force,* and *Yank.* Still others appeared in the journals and newspapers of the civilian press.

Having found these photographs was one thing; knowing what to do with them was quite another. At first I thought they would make a cute dog book. I justified this sentiment for several reasons: Dog photography has enjoyed quite a renaissance in recent years, and these dogs were certainly cute. Why not display this collection with an emphasis on the canines themselves, I thought. But then again, I thought not. It wasn't just the dogs at work in these photos. There was something else here, something that I noticed only when I viewed the collection as a whole. Let me explain.

Today, World War II is best known by the names of the battles and the turning points that determined the outcome, but it wasn't that way 50 years ago. Peleliu, Bastogne, Iwo Jima, and Malmedy? They were words that tangled up on a farmer's tongue, but not so the names of the boys that were fighting in those areas—the Jacks, Arthurs, Miltons, and Matthews. Back then, the war was about fathers, sons, and husbands, not pinpoints on maps, a nation's ideologies, or epic battles.

Taken as a whole, these pictures remind us that while the war certainly transformed America, it didn't transform us. We remained a caring nation of quiet, keep-to-ourselves kinds of towns that prayed the boys would be home soon.

These captions help us see America in the 1940s, though not directly. A distinct tone and manner suffuses this collection and through it, there is a subtle portrait of America. Before the war, people gave little thought to international politics; few had traveled further from home than the distance required to visit a cousin one county over. But World War II changed all that. In the blink of an eye, Pearl Harbor was in flames and just as quickly, hundreds of thousands of men were enlisting. They left their homes, were processed, sent to

Bullseye. Bombardier training center. The magic was mascot photography. Dogs and soldiers. One well-composed photo spoke to the hearts of a nation better than pages of written reassurances.

basic training, and then shipped on to learn their specialties. They learned to use rifles, bazookas, and flame throwers, perhaps to fly fighters, or to man ships or submarines. And then, within a week of their training's end, they were sent to war in China, Burma, England, North Africa, Australia, the Marshalls, Italy, or the Aleutians. They left on destroyers, aircraft carriers, troop transports, and submarines. They used weapons called P-51 Mustangs, B-17 Flying Fortresses, Sherman tanks, and PT boats.

It was such a long way from Louisville, Maryville, Muncie, Eugene, Camden, Butte, and all the hollers and the hundreds of small towns of America. But through it all, the soldiers were still the boys, and America, while shaken by the war, didn't lose its compassion or its maternal instincts. The evidence abounds in these photographs. As one poignant wartime caption noted, "Millions of American men are overseas fighting the enemy, but if any proof were needed that they're still pretty much the same kind of fellow that left home, this photo adds a convincing touch. Dogs and boys go together—and no matter where they are, when they can, boys take their pets along."

Some historical notes are in order. The pictures in this book were taken between 1941 and late 1945. Most of them were taken in a theater of combat, but some were taken at stateside training bases. Note that this is not a book about "war dogs," that is, dogs trained to function in the war itself. War dogs were instrumental on the battlegrounds, particularly in the Pacific, but they've been thoroughly chronicled by other authors and, accordingly, are not the focus of this book. Nonetheless, I felt compelled to include a few; when you see them (pages 122 and 125) you will understand why.

Although most of the pets adopted by soldiers were dogs, in the Far Pacific, dogs were rare. The need for companionship, however, was not. Thus, out there on the hot jungle islands, surrounded by endless horizons of ocean, battle-hardened Marines adopted cats, goats, donkeys, parrots, monkeys, roosters, cheetah, frogs, and even a snake as their mascots. Some wonderful pictures thus evolved. Although I prefer dogs, I would adopt the cat on page 80 in a second!

Note also that none of the dogs in this book are the official mascots of the military academies nor of any of the high institutions of the war years. Yes, most of them *became* official mascots of their units and were duly vested with imaginative rank and honor; that was inevitable. But there are no glamour dogs here. The overwhelming majority of these animals are mutts; simple, low-bred mutts, frightened by the guns, hungry, and separated from their homes—dogs not much different from the boys who took them in and gave them a place to sleep.

To the preceding generalization, I have made one exception. I included President Roosevelt's dog (page 14). Roosevelt meant so much to the men and to the nation that if Roosevelt did it, the nation knew it was all right. For those who considered adopting dogs, Roosevelt was their stamp of approval.

Some final notes: All branches of the armed forces produced dog photography, but they were quite different in the way they went about it. The Signal Corps photos, for instance, are restrained and reserved, and almost always without humor. Furthermore, their pictures tend to lack artistic composition or intimacy; they are hurried, and they are, by far, the most journalistic photos of the lot. That said, there are many fine examples of buddy photography in this record group. I recommend, in particular, the picture of a soldier and his dog on page 12. The young man's tired eyes speak volumes about the misery of war, while the dog he holds so hungrily says even more about staying sane amidst it all. Of the entire collection, this is my favorite.

The Air Force, which was then part of the Army, albeit with the swashbuckle of a fighter pilot, was at times downright vaudevillian in its approach. Look at Boots on page 34, or Bullseye on page 11 (inspired, no doubt, by the television character Petie of *Our Gang*). You can't help but appreciate the antics that preceded these photos, nor can you stop smiling as you view the results.

The Marine Corps had its own correspondents and the selections from their archives represent a considerable part of this book, largely because the Marines had some of the most unusual war pets, including the rifle-squeezing snake. That said, I should add this. Despite the no-nonsense, hard-nosed reputation of the Corps, you will find some of the most compassionate pictures of the lot right here. The Marines may be the "proud and the few," but they certainly have an unflinching sense of what they are which, in a word, is mortal. In an odd way, more than the others, the Marines' photography seems to celebrate the soldier as an individual.

Without doubt, the best of the dog photography, and the best of the captions, comes from the Coast Guard. Their material was the most enthusiastic and the least restrained of the bunch. Most know of the Coast Guard's participation in World War II; few know how extensive it was. Coast Guardsmen ran Higgins Boats onto the

Tojo the monkey and his pal stopped to pose for a photo while on shore liberty. Not all mascots were dogs, particularly in the Far Pacific. But it didn't matter.
Monkey, cat, cookodo—a pet was a pet.

Franklin D. Roosevelt and his dogs. The commander in chief taking his dogs with him gave unofficial sanction to the field practice of adopting animals as mascots.

D-Day beaches at Normandy, piloted troop convoys across the Atlantic, captained transport ships, undertook evacuations, and steered landing craft onto almost every beach that America hit in both the European and Pacific theaters.

The Coast Guard stood at the tip of the spear, yet, judging from their dog photography, they kept a strong sense of their own humanity. Read some of the tongue-in-cheek captions—they bristle with well-timed, double entendres. "Salty has been promoted to Bones First Mate," and "the chow is dog-gone good" for a mascot named Hobo.

In presenting this collection, I considered the journalistic environment of World War II. Because the war dominated the news in most newspapers and magazines, it seemed appropriate to mix in selected combat photos with this collection, which I have done, albeit sparingly.

Where they were available, I have also included the original captions and when I did, I left them untouched. Any effort to edit them invariably drained flavor from the original composition. However, when I did edit, I did so only to eliminate repetitive detail or the sometimes tedious lists of ranks. Not all photos had captions, though. To differentiate the captions I added from the wartime captions, my words appear in italics.

Max, by the way, appears on page 16. Max, in fact, jumped out of an airplane five times and did win his parachute wings. Even the regiment's commanding officer, Colonel James M. Gavin, got into the spirit of things. He pinned Max's wings on his . . . err, chest.

So, here they are, the good men of that great generation going through the heartless motions of war, with their buddy, a dog. Without this magical animal, we would just see soldiers, but because of it, we see again the young men, the sons and fathers and husbands—our parents and grandparents—as they were, back when an entire nation was consumed with the unspeakable job of fighting World War II.

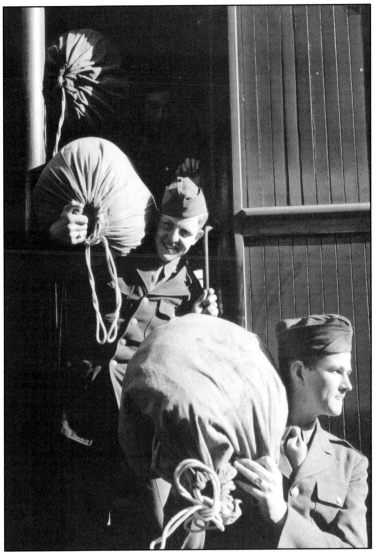

Shipping out, 1942.

CHAPTER 1

Dogs and Dogfaces
Mascots of the Army

The Signal Corps, being the Army's communication's division, went everywhere the Army went. Members of the Signal Corps trailed just a day or so behind the major engagements, walking through the camps and foxholes afterward, camera and notepad in hand. They were on the invasion beaches of D-Day, and on the islands of the Pacific. They were at the air bases in England, at the training bases in America, and even on the troop transports crossing the Atlantic.

As a result, the Signal Corps collections offer a tremendous range of mascot photography. Depending on where it was taken, some of the photography is playful, like the shots of Max, who was photographed at a training base in the States. Other images are decidedly journalistic; most of the Signal Corps photographs are from the front lines and are thus tinged with the underlying seriousness of war. Indeed, in this collection one sees the only photos taken of a soldier and dog together in combat. Of all the captions of the mascot genre, the Signal Corps' are the most austere and matter-of-fact of the bunch. They make only scant reference to where the photograph was taken or what the circumstances were. Indeed, three lines was a long caption for the Signal Corps, the notable exceptions being those issued from the training bases.

The mascot of the 505th Parachute Infantry, Max was a full-fledged paratrooper having jumped the necessary five times to qualify. Max, like all parachutists, was a volunteer. Fort Benning, Georgia.

Junior with correspondent at Camp Lucky Strike, Le Havre, France, 1945.

Gearing up, 101st Airborne, 1944, England. The 101st and the 82nd spearheaded Operation Overlord—the D-Day invasion of France.

Jumper saying good-bye to paratrooper George
Vespa of Wilkinsburg, Pennsylvania, as his master
departs for the Luzon Island, Philippines, jump.

Private Jesse Fennell and his dog, Dud, waiting for transportation to their new camp in France. His outfit, the 101st Airborne Division, had just been relieved by Canadian troops after two months of steady combat.

Men of M Company, 337th Infantry Regiment, cleaning up in front of their dugouts. February 1945.

The mascot of the 766th Light Ordnance Company has just made a new home amid the truck tires and has had a litter of pups. Corporal Joseph Gabriele, left, of Philadelphia, Pennsylvania, and Staff Sergeant Troy Greene, Metter, Georgia, are shown inspecting the new comers. St. Nazaire Sector, France.

Two medics of the 95th Infantry Division take a break with their pet dog, Chippie. Left to right, Henry Ertzweiler, Wausau, Wisconsin, and Private First Class J. H. David, Clarks Hill, Indiana. They found Chippie while fighting in the Rhine River area.

Private First Class Calvin J. Fontana, North Bergen, New Jersey, with pet, Ginger. Seventh Army, 44th Infantry Division, Haiming, Austria.

Infantry men of the 26th Division wait in trucks in Ottweiler, Germany, before moving up. Technical Specialist 4 Mediroa holds the mascot, Little Joe.

Crouching low for maximum concealment, troops of the 89th Infantry Division, 3rd Army, cross the Rhine River at Oberwesel, as German bullets whiz by overhead. March 1945.

Private Frank Hancock of Monticello, Kentucky, a member of an antiaircraft battalion in France, plays with the gun crew's dog, General. General has been with the crew since the African campaign. Private Hancock has been overseas 2 1/2 years.

Corporal Frederick Scatko and Staff Sergeant Peter Murray, 9th US Army, play with their mascot, Cognac, whom they found as a pup in Normandy. He has been traveling with them ever since.

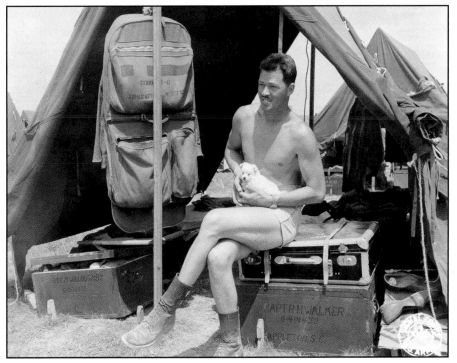

Captain Ralph Walker of Appleton, South Carolina, is seen outside his tent at Camp Miami in Chalons, France. The captain fought from Normandy to the heart of the Reich. At Leipzig, he picked up the mascot seen here, a German spitz puppy named Buddy.

Private Calvin Fontana, North Bergen, New Jersey, with pet Ginger. 7th Army, 44th MP Platoon, Haiming, Austria.

Staff Sergeant Joe Kodachrome, mascot of a photographic unit somewhere in the European Theater of Operations, stands up to the bar for his nightly ration of milk and bitters. Running Horse pub, London, England, March, 1944.

Company pet Leipzig, found when the solders entered Leipzig, Germany.

With his overseas hat perched jauntily on his head, Mike, a boxer, sits forlornly for the photographer, somewhere in France, 1945.

CHAPTER 2:

Dog Fights
Mascots of the Army Air Forces

There is a saying among aviators meant to contrast their attitudes with those of their comrades in the Army and the Navy: "Pilots have more fun." True or not, it seems to be in evidence as far their dog photography goes. From the very first to the very last, humor suffuses the U.S. Army Air Forces' approach to settings and situations. U.S. Army Air Forces photographers all but dressed their four-legged buddies in skirts before snapping a photo and sending it back to the hometown newspapers. Not that the other services didn't have a sense of humor, it's just that the U.S. Army Air Forces excelled in sight pranks. For example, Boots appeared with his goggles and parachute on, and in another, Skippy was made ready for any enemy attack by equipping him with an oxygen mask.

U.S. Army Air Forces captions are both informative and playful. Moreover, they tend to tell a story. They are sprinkled with wonderful detail and odd facts. Boots wasn't just simply dressed for flight; we read *why* Boots was dressed up, where he went, and what he did.

By far, the most frequent type of buddy photography in the U.S. Army Air Forces files was an air crew and its dog. Such photography tended to be repetitive and a bit insipid, much like the snapshot of a softball team or some such activity, but one example is included that, in terms of composition and nose art on the bomber, was one of the best. One important note about this collection: The U.S. Army Air Forces was reluctant to identify the people in its photographs, particularly if they were pilots. This was consistent with other policies then in effect to protect pilots in the event they were shot down over enemy territory. Who knew what foreign agent might be culling through American papers? It served no purpose to compromise a pilot's already thin chances of escape by broadcasting how many missions he had flown or how many "kills" he had.

Nine members of the crew of the B-17 bomber Ole Miss *pose with their mascot.*

Waist gunner as seen from another B-17 during a mission over Germany.

Trixie is the mascot of the 16th Observation Squadron. The dog is equipped with her own parachute. The chute was rebuilt from a discarded flare-chute by Sergeant John Patrick and the parachute riggers department.

Boss of the hangar line, that's Boots, or more formally, Texas Ranger, mascot of the Military Police Detail at Randolph Field, Texas. In reality, Boots is rated as canine copilot on the prowl car, but since acquiring his specially built flight equipment, he's not above trying to steal a ride in a basic training plane. Boots is nearing his fourth birthday and, despite his fierce scowl, is really an amiable guy.

A fresh-scrubbed innocence shines on the face of this pilot even in the midst of war. America can thank Lieutenant Russell Stump for getting rid of a Nazi plane.

A member of the 7th Air Force Fighter Command ground unit reads one of the pocket-edition books to while away the time aboard ship. He is en route to the beachhead on Iwo Jima, 1945.

When this caption first appeared in the February 1944 issue of Air Force magazine, the pilot's name was intentionally left out. Instead, written in the voice of the dog, the caption simply declares, "Take good care of yourself!"

Here is Skippy, the unofficial crew member of a big Flying Fortress in the Northwest African theater.

Skippy, a four-year-old pit bull pointer, was such a well-loved mascot among the bomber crews in North Africa that one of the pilots painted his picture on his B-17 Flying Fortress. This was more than noteworthy, as most crews chose art of the leggy, female variety. Skippy was more than a mascot, though. He was an unofficial crew member, logging over 200 hours of flying time, a trip across the Atlantic, and actual combat missions over Tunisia and Sicily. Requiring the same accouterments as any member of the crew, Skippy had his own oxygen mask rigged to fit his muzzle.

Skippy, mascot of B-17 *Our Gang*, is one of the most pampered mascots in England. He lives the life of the 324th Bomb Squadron, 91st Bomb Group, of which his master is a member, 1943.

Any animal was fair game
when it came time to
adopt pets as mascots.
This monkey mascot is
perched on the spinner of
a P-40 of the 16th Fighter
Squadron, 51st Fighter
Group, in China, 1942.

This photo from the European theater shows Brigadier General Robert Travis, combat wing commander, addressing the men of the 379th Bomb Group.

Brigadier General Truman Landon, commanding general, VII Bomber Command (Pacific Theater of Operations), and his female dachshund, Herman, just before taking off for new headquarters at Kwajalein in the Gilbert Islands.

Two men of the 7th Air Force Fighter Command ground crew play cards.

First appearing in *Yank* magazine in 1944, this photo shows Major Bill "Red" Benedict, Captain Charles Leaf, and the mascot of their 5th Army Thunderbolt squadron in Italy.

Lieutenant Colonel Goldenberger and his dog standing beside his plane, *Honey Chile*. England, 1945.

A member of the 3rd Bomb Division's 452nd Bomb Group is a veteran of the air war but draws no flight pay. Blondie is shown here with two members of her B-17 Flying Fortress *Up'n Front*. Blondie adopted her crewmates when they were in Italy. Modifying an oxygen mask for the dog, the airmen flew her back from Italy to England, and she has since made frequent Fortress flights.

The tired faces of this returning B-17 crew are a reminder that mascots served more than just the home front. What better way to relieve the weariness of a mission, the stress of battle, than to tousle the fur of a dog?

Stuka, the mascot of the *Memphis Belle* crew,
cools off in the shade of the plane. England, 1943.

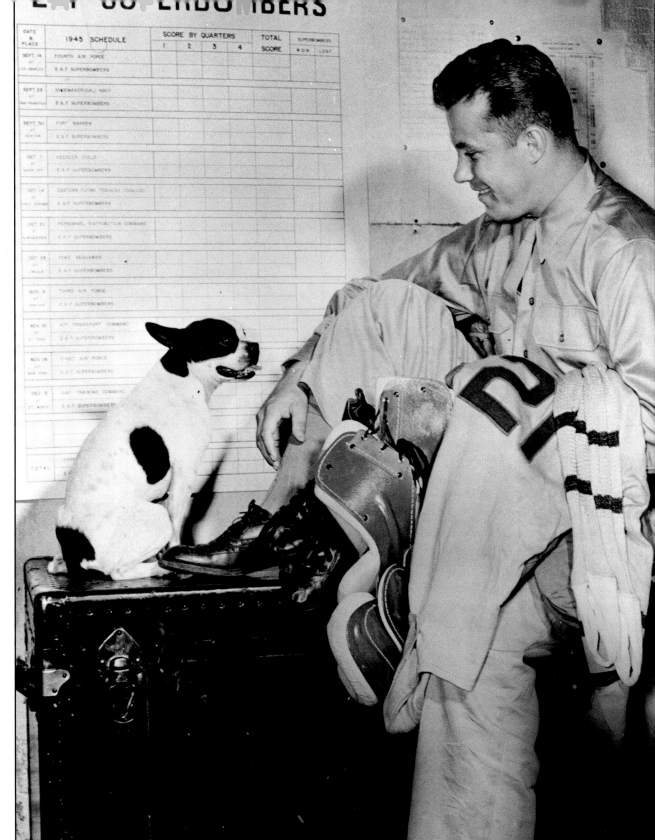

Jerry, bull terrier of the Second Air Force, greets Frank Sinkwich, former Georgia All-American and 1944 National League most valuable player.

Though still a puppy, Tracer had been hanging around airplanes so long at the aerial gunnery school in Harlingen, Texas, that he didn't mind lounging on the ammo box of a Browning machine gun. Although Tracer had the run of the base and this trainee appears to be ready to fly out to gunnery practice over the Gulf of Mexico, Tracer never flew out with the guys.

CHAPTER 3

Salty Dogs
Dogs of the U.S. Navy

Each branch of the military had its own way of filing photography and as a result, some files were easier to research than others. One of the easiest was the U.S. Navy's. For unknown reasons, each of the Navy's press photos was luxuriously mounted on white cardboard and captioned in a space immediately to the left. The results made handling photos a breeze, an important consideration when thousands of photos are involved. The same is not true, however, for the organization of these photos.

Finding buddy photography in the Navy records was difficult indeed. Not that they weren't there. Ships had mascots, and Navy pilots had mascots. In fact, the first buddy photo in the Navy collections appeared within a matter of minutes of my initial foray. But they were terribly slow in coming, and that had everything to do with what I would generously call haphazard organization. The content of a given box would jump from one topic to the other without a single divider or forewarning. One photo might be from Pearl Harbor, the next of flight operations on Guadalcanal, and the next a landing in Italy—with two buddy photographs mixed in.

The selection of buddy photography in this section focuses almost exclusively on ships, and the ship's company. Here are dogs in some of the most unusual places— in torpedo tubes, on the barrel of a gun, waiting for the buddies to come ashore, with a flight crew. The Navy records also provided some of the most humorous mascot photos of the lot. Some of them are included in the final chapter of the book, "Who Said I'm a Dog?"

Navy sailor plays with Salty.

Two sailors on the USS Milletle *take a break with their mascot in 1945.*

Explaining a photo problem to the lab mascot, Pistol, 1945.

The guard on a merchant vessel fill the munitions "ready box" as their mascot, Arab, watches, 1943.

On the conning tower of an American submarine tied up at an unidentified base, this sailor is reading the comics while his mascot pants in the shade.

Determined to follow his pals to the beach, Hobo hopped onto a tank that is about to be hoisted into a landing craft.

H. W. Kenworth, after having been on 7,000 war patrol miles in Japanese waters, demonstrates the size of his submarine's torpedo tubes. To make the point even clearer, Kenworth cradled the buddy who withstood enemy depth charges and shelling right along with his master.

Flash is all set for takeoff. Here he is seen looking things over from the lap of copilot Ensign John Yakich.

Flash, the terrier mascot of this air wing of Harpoons flying against installations near their Aleutians base. Flash works hard at his job and goes along on all flights.

This mascot pup greets a sub crew returning after extended patrol in enemy waters.

Down in the Southwest Pacific, parrots vie with dogs as mascots for Uncle Sam's seafaring fighters. Here a picturesque Coast Guardsman, with his beard and earring, gives his hitchhiking pal, Jockey, a lift as he goes about his duties.

In the foreground, the crew of PCE 851 search the skies for more enemy planes, as an LST burns in the background after a hit by a Japanese suicide plane.

Snuffy, a three-month-old pet of Ensign Clifford Ramsey at the Naval Air Station, Kodiak, Alaska, December, 1943.

Mascot of LC 1947, Fossil works the
colored signal light near Guam.

Sparky, on patrol in the Atlantic safeguarding the shipping lanes against a possible revival of sub action, snaps his eyes and ears on an approaching vessel.

An aircraft carrier lists to port, somewhere in the Pacific.

Always standing in line, that's the life of a Coast Guardsman, and Barney gets no special treatment.

Navy sailors gather around a drone and a dog named Rosie.

B-Day for Steamboat. It's bath day for the mascot of an assault transport somewhere in the Pacific. Steamboat takes his dunking under protest and wonders why his pal goes out of his way to make him miserable.

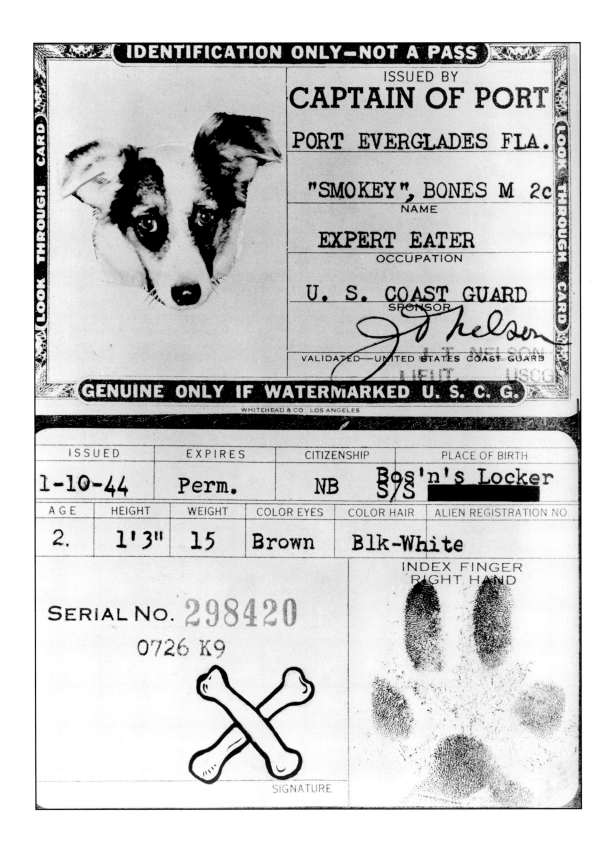

CHAPTER 4

Dog Tags
Mascots of the U.S. Coast Guard

The Coast Guard war correspondents elevated buddy photography to high art. There is the consistent use of play-on-words as a dramatic device in the captions. Writers cleverly wove their way through common nautical terminology, then accented their prose with paws, barks, and other four-legged references.

There is also is a great deal of story-telling here. Many captions are sparse, but a great many more tell tall tales that stretched the imagination of the writer and thoroughly engage the reader. Surely there were easier ways to write a caption, but none more heartwarming than these.

This collection goes as far as any to reveal the gentle side of we Americans in the 1940s. To have written such captions required a native compassion but to have *known to write such captions* was to know the audience at home was also compassionate. The totality of the Coast Guard material—the composition of the photo, the innocent animal, the innocent young boys, the backdrop of war, the playful captions, even the inclusion of names and addresses of the soldiers—makes this the most historically significant collection of all the photos. It is more than buddy photography. It is a window into a time and a place that's now long gone.

In this series, dogs that survived gun battles and submarine encounters and escaped German or Japanese captors all appear. Like their counterparts in the U.S. Army Air Forces, Coasties couldn't resist propping their dogs appropriate to the situation. Thus, dogs with kerchiefs, holding forks, even shielding their eyes with sunglasses all grace this collection.

When two tankers off the Florida coast collided and caught fire, 88 men lost their lives. After Coast Guardsmen doused the flames, the only living creature they found was a dog, whom they named Smokey. After several months the crew promoted her to Bones' Mate, Second Class, and issued an official identification card giving her occupation as expert eater. The card was signed with Smokey's paw prints.

Most ships' dogs have no truck with the gold braids, but Fido, mascot of an LST, is a democratic cuss. Officers and enlisted are all the same to him. Here, he visits with Army Lieutenant Stanley K. Jackson of Jersey City, New Jersey, as the LST moves upon Morotai Island in the far Pacific.

Screech, the puppy mascot on a cutter on convoy duty, is always ready when mess call is sounded. "The more mess, the better," thinks Screech. Here he accepts a morsel from the tray of one of his pals, Boatswain's Mate Carmine Giangrasso. Share and share alike, eh, pal?

Sinbad is a fighting dog from a fighting ship—most of the time. When the cutter ran into a U-boat pack, it depth charged six of the submarines and sank the last by ramming it. Sinbad slept through it all at his battle station—in a bunk. When the ship is in port, though, Sinbad upholds his reputation by taking on anything on paws. His five years of sea duty have made him a crafty fighter, indeed.

Soogie, the mascot of a Coast Guard-manned LCI operating in French waters, had been on station a long time—three years since he came aboard in Galveston, Texas. He gave the photographer a grim look as he posed before the likeness of a fighting Donald Duck insignia on his ship. If Soogie looked a bit tired, it was because by late 1944 he had already been part of three invasions—Sicily, Salerno, and Normandy. His Coast Guard mates gave him a rating—Morale Builder, First Class.

USS Wasp, *September 15, 1942. Torpedoed off Savo Island (Guadalcanal) the* Wasp *was abandoned at 1520 hours, sinking later that day.*

He's just an old snooze hound—Tugboat, the mascot of the Coast Guard cargo ship running fighting men and supplies to the island battle fronts of the Far Pacific. Next to sleepin', Tugboat prefers eatin' and he does all right in the ship's galley. Here Tug dreams of a porterhouse steak in the arms of Keinard Post, of Honolulu, Hawaii.

Coast Guard fighting ships have dogs holding down the important duties of mascot, but there is one ship plying the combat waters with a frisky kitten at the helm. Here she is, Midnight, in the hands of Coast Guardsman Elmer Barnes.

The brown-and-white pup under the machinist mate's right arm had the bad luck to be on the beach in Normandy as the invasion of Europe began on June 6, 1944. Bullets zinged past his floppy ears and artillery rounds exploded all around. Cherbourg—the name given to him by his American rescuers—didn't know what to do. Then an LST powered into the beach and lowered its ramp. As Yankee soldiers piled out, the frightened pup ran up the ramp between their legs, and found refuge in the cavernous interior. From that moment on, the ship had two mascots— Cherbourg on the left, and Boots, a German Shepherd owned by one of the Coast Guardsmen.

An unidentified Coast Guardsman surveys the beach at Saipan, while a captive chicken tugs at its bonds behind his back.

Jo Ann is always curious about the goings-on on her ship. A coiled hawser on the deck grabbed her interest . . . and then her leg. So Jo Ann just snoozed until one of her shipmates freed her from her trap.

This dachshund has sniffed the air in the South Pacific and off the coast of North Africa. Monsoons and trade winds only add to his appetite as he pads about the deck, keeping his pals happy.

Queenie, the mascot of a supply ship in the Pacific Theater manned by the Coast Guard, stood her watch at a gun station, peering through her sunglasses, ready to bark at anything arousing her suspicions. With a rating of SPAR, first class, Queenie had the run of the foc'sle and bridge.

Left: When on duty, Blackout, the satin-coated mascot of an LCI (Landing Craft, Infantry) wore a life jacket made by one of his pals—just in case. The ship had been in action in the Mediterranean, and there was no telling when Blackout might be dunked in the water—so he was prepared. Blackout was indeed a veteran. The three battle stars on his service ribbon commemorated the beaches he'd hit—Sicily, Italy, and Normandy.

Right: Pepper is a salty veteran of Pacific invasions. A mascot aboard a Coast Guard invasion transport, this frolicsome pup has barked his way through half a dozen assaults against Japanese island beaches, including Tarawa, Saipan, Okinawa, and Luzon. Here he is—sure enough—off the shore of Peleliu with two of his pals, Edward Lynch of Freeport, New York, and Erwin Enos of Bellmore, New York.

Mr. Chips was picked up by a crew member of the USS *Harris*, a Navy transport, and became the ship's mascot. The holder of a health record, identification card, and a dog tag, Mr. Chips participated in the attack on Attu. Mugging for the camera, Chips looks at a Japanese gas mask found on Kiska.

Left: Mike, a mascot mutt aboard a destroyer escort in the North Atlantic, waits patiently for the word to dig in. The napkin, of course, is phony; seagoing dogs scoff at anything as high-toned as a napkin. Mike specializes in ham bones, but he will just as gladly gobble soup and celery, only to yip for second helpings!

Salty, a mascot on an assault transport, didn't have anybody fooled. Whenever the bos'n piped "all hands to swab down," Salty hopped up on the nearest boom or gun barrel to watch and bark wisecracks at his shipmates. Salty was a first-class gold-brick, but the men loved him anyway.

Things are just "sew, sew" at sea. A Coast Guardsman is a versatile chap, adept with ropes, winches, and even the needle. Here Harold Adams does some "fancy work" on a piece of canvas, while the curious puppy mascot, aptly named Nosey, climbed on his shoulder to see what was going on.

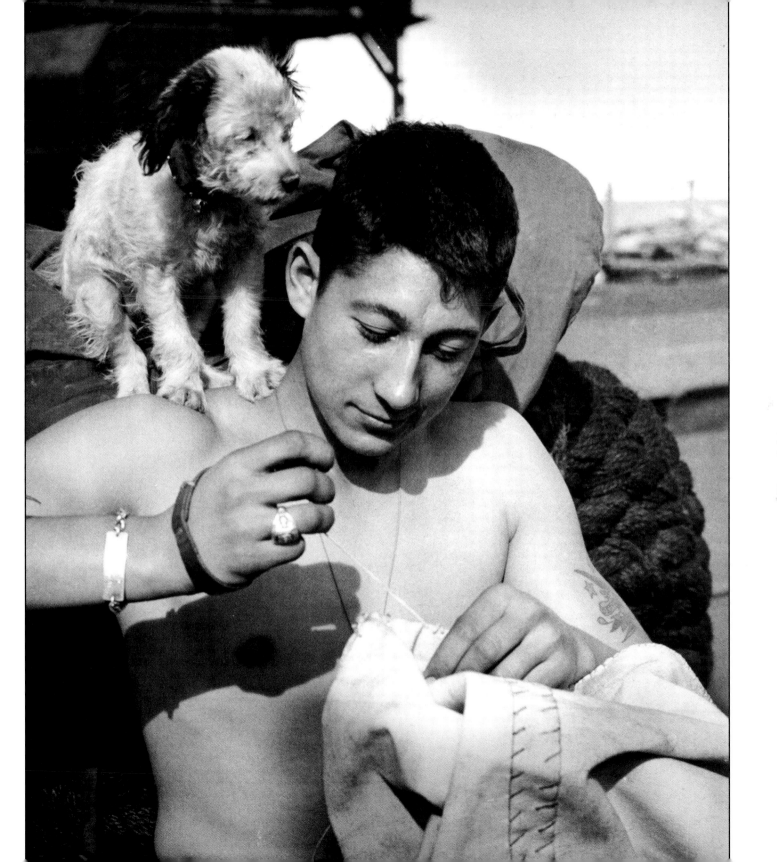

Mascot of a Coast Guard combat cutter, Sparky is ready to abandon ship if the emergency should arise. The sea dog wears a life jacket carefully tailored by his shipmates. A veteran of long service aboard this Atlantic sub hunter, Sparky knows the smell of battle. He has seen an enemy sub go to the bottom.

Saki, a black cocker mascot of a Coast Guard-manned LST, was in there with his shipmates when American forces attacked and finally conquered the Japanese bastion on Biak Island in the Southwest Pacific. Here Saki is shown with one of his pals, Seaman First Class Kenneth Smith, Clawson, Michigan, on the deck of the LST before an antiaircraft gun.

As Coast Guard Lieutenant Commander Jack Dixon scanned the deck of a sinking ship, he found only this forlorn puppy, apparently abandoned by the crew. As the sea rose over the gunwales and started flooding the ship, the frightened pooch climbed the stairs to save himself. Commander Dixon rescued the grateful animal, but not before taking this heart-rending picture of a sad, scared pup. This photo won first honors at a 1940s showing at the National Press Club in Washington D.C.

Has anybody seen Kelly? Yeah, that's Kelly sittin' up there on the aft gun barrel. H.E. (High Explosive) Kelly is the mascot of an invasion transport now helping to kick the daylights out of the Japanese in the Far Pacific. Kelly has served on two oceans and only been ashore twice in his life—on the docks of Honolulu and on the battle-scarred beach of Eniwetok. He's down on the ship's muster roll as a gunner's mate, second class, promoted two jumps for his exceptional barking at Saipan.

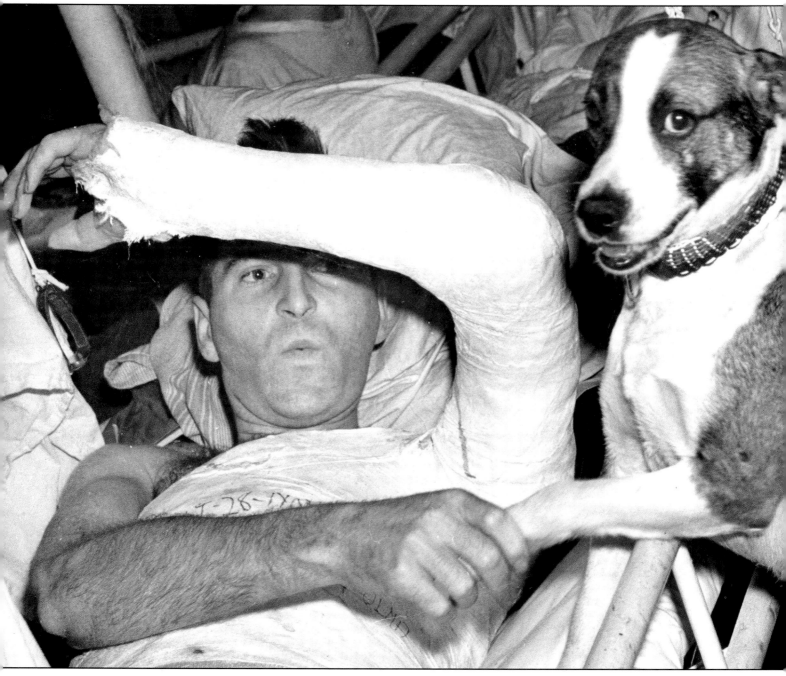

His name used to be Half Hitch but the wounded boys started calling him Doc Sunshine. Doc assigned himself to the cheer-up duty in the morale-upping division aboard a transport. Doc strolls from bunk to bunk shaking paws and giving all the boys that things-are-getting-better-every-day feeling.

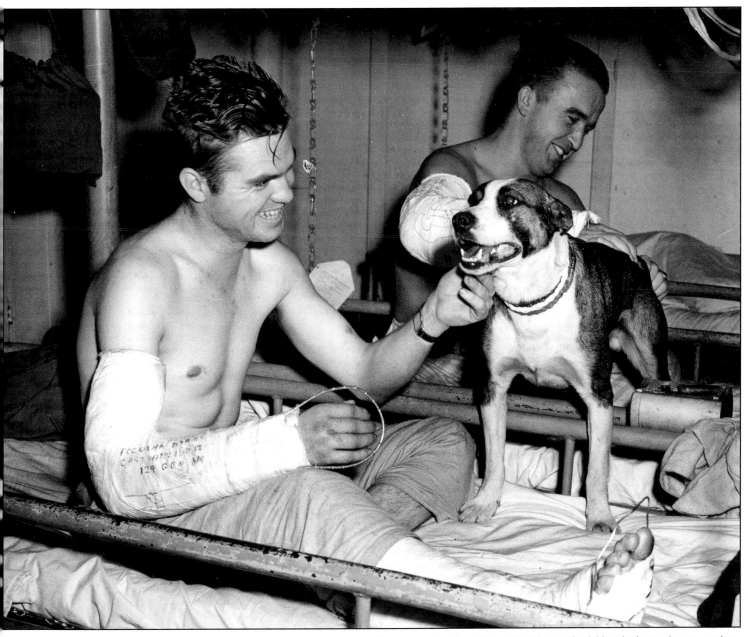

All day long, Doc Sunshine makes his rounds visiting the boys who are coming home with their arms and legs in casts and their heads in bandages. He makes 'em forget the war and break into smiles. Here Doc drops in on Private First Class Harold Keel of Tennessee City, Tennessee, who got in the way of some German machine gun fire.

Doc Sunshine played no favorites on his troop transport. He liked everybody—both the soldiers heading to Europe as reinforcements and the soldiers coming back from Europe as casualties. His headquarters was a K rations box, from which he dispensed good cheer.

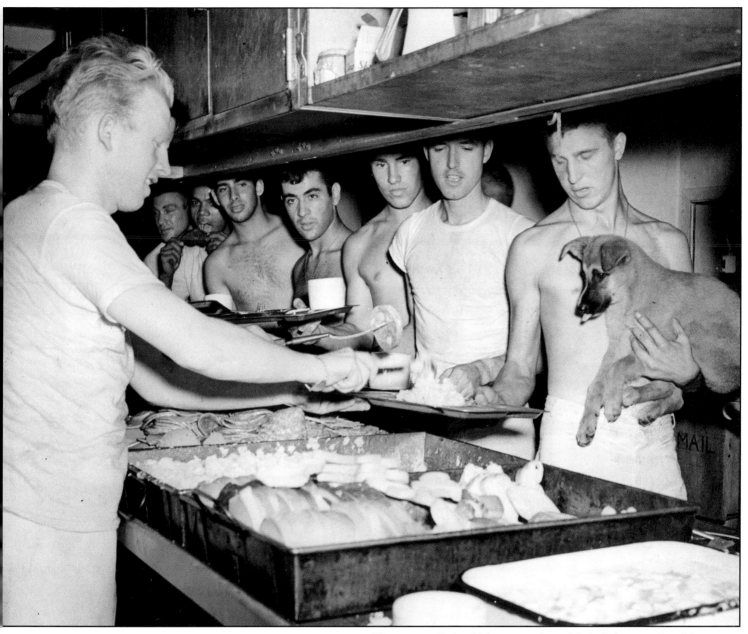

Wherever you find a ship's crew, you're certain to find a mascot, and these Coast Guardsmen are no exception. Lined up for evening chow somewhere at sea, Mutt is first in line. Tongue lolling and drooling in anticipation, Mutt stares avidly as his master's tray is piled high.

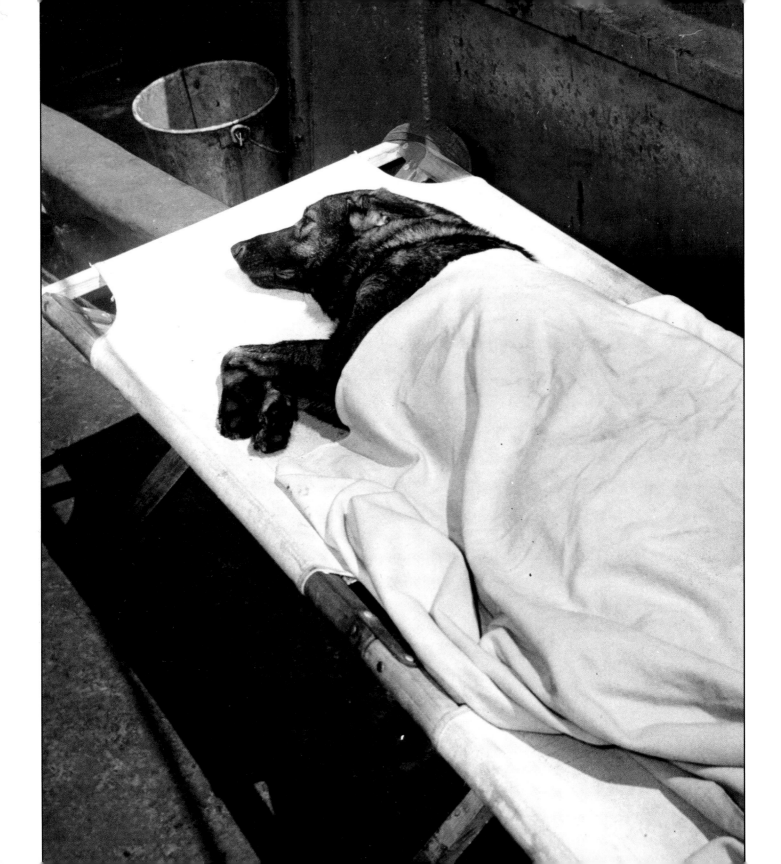

Bunky, a casualty of the battles on Peleliu, is seen here in the sickbay. Mascots were no safer than the men they served, not in the heat of battle.

Jack is lost in sleep on a cutter, somewhere in the Pacific combat area.

With a bandaged eye, Sparky returned from a Marshall Islands beach a veteran of battle and a hero of the war. Going in with the Marines off an assault ship, Sparky did a good job of barking at the Japanese before an injury got him carried back to the ship. After the battle, still carrying his own rations, he swapped war stories with his buddies.

Knobby, the mascot on an 83-foot rescue cutter, found himself a part of history by being on board when the ship was part of the armada that sailed across the English Channel to Normandy on D-Day, June 6, 1944. Wearing his specially made life preserver, Knobby stayed right in there, barking orders as the beachhead was established, and he witnessed the rescue of over 750 American and Allied invaders on that fateful day.

Right: Either romping or snuggling, these happy mutts aboard hospital ships are just what the doctor ordered for injured American servicemen. These mascot pups brightened the day of some Marines, hit by Japanese fire in the invasion of Peleliu.

Left: Barnacle Bill poses with his Coast Guard partner's hat. This is just for fun, but the important work of guarding our coast is not in fun. These dogs and the armed sentries of the Coast Guard take their responsibilities very seriously.

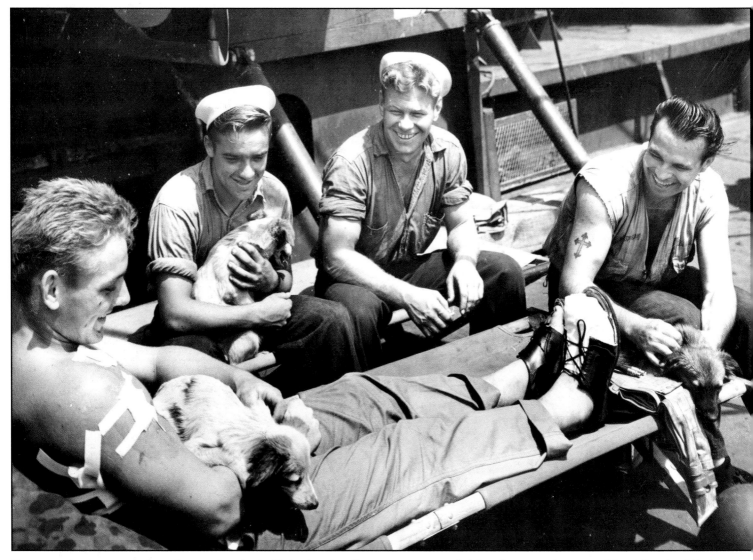

These seagoing pups are the best of companions for the Yankee invaders. Two mascots express their happiness over the return of Coast Guard and Marine invaders from the roaring beaches of Peleliu.

Roaming his watch in his custom-made sweater, Sparky, the floppy-eared mascot of a combat cutter, got mixed up with a high doorsill in a rough sea. With a painfully injured forepaw, Sparky limped to sickbay under his own power. Even though a sympathetic pharmacist's mate dressed his wound, Sparky was a casualty for weeks.

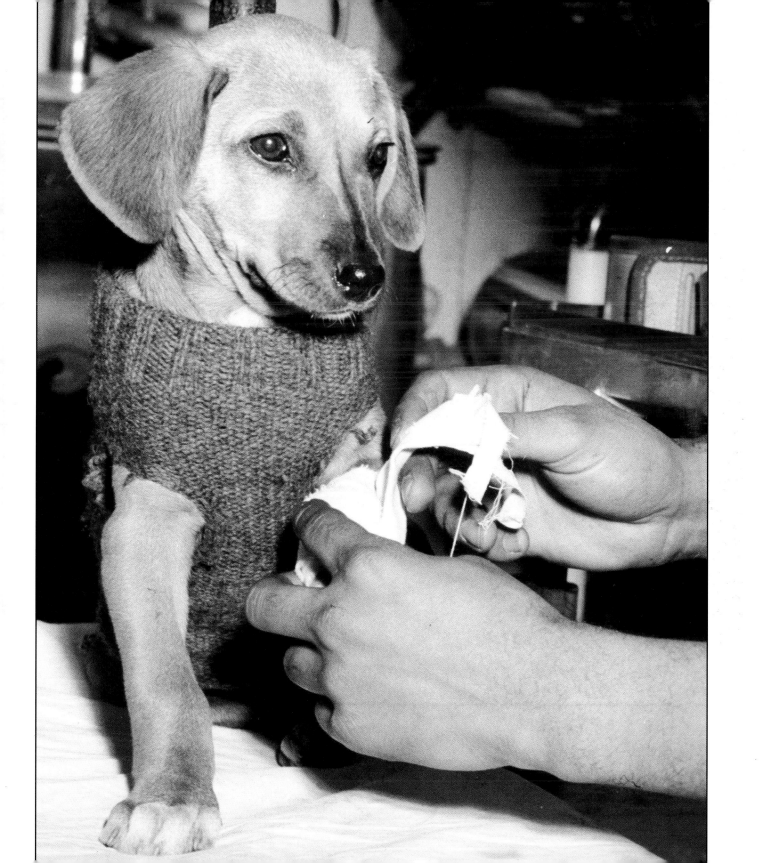

Invader, the boys call him. He went ashore with his shipmates in Sicily and again at Salerno. Here Invader is shown before the big push against the French coast. Unperturbed and always ready, this shaggy LCI mascot is a Coast Guardsman from the tip of his nose to the end of his tail.

Not only does Rusty Robin have his own life jacket, but he also has his own battle station aboard his Coast Guard combat cutter: in the skipper's shower. Rusty Robin recently returned from a two-year tour of duty on the North Atlantic, during which time he never set paw on land.

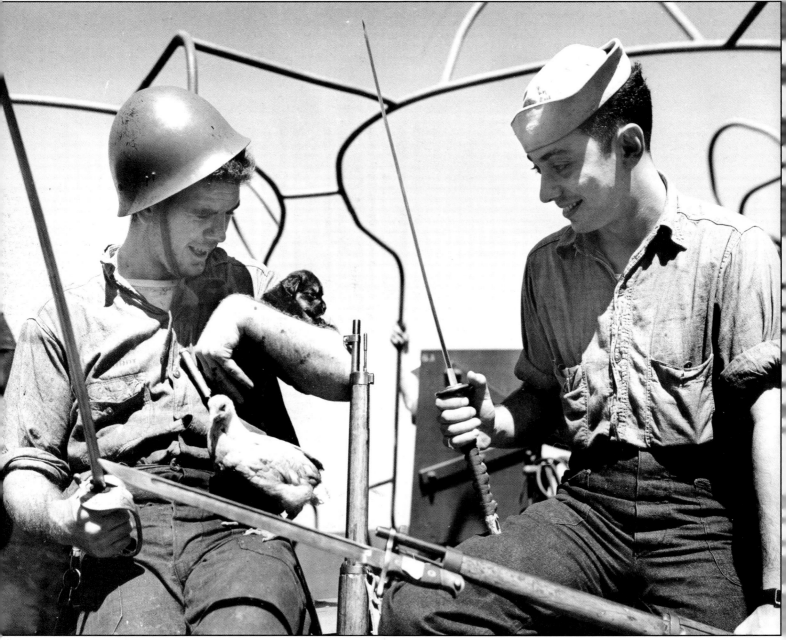

Homebound from the South Pacific in 1945, these two Coast Guardsmen show off some of the Japanese swords and guns they carted away from the invasion beaches. With them are two of the ship's mascots—a chicken named Japo and a dog named Joe. Joe was actually born on ship, making him a seaman for life. The infamous story of Japo was known by everyone in the Seventh Fleet—how she suddenly came cackling and fluttering out of a Marshall Islands beach assault, dashing up the ramp of the landing craft and throwing herself into the arms of the crew, as if to say, "I'm not Japanese!"

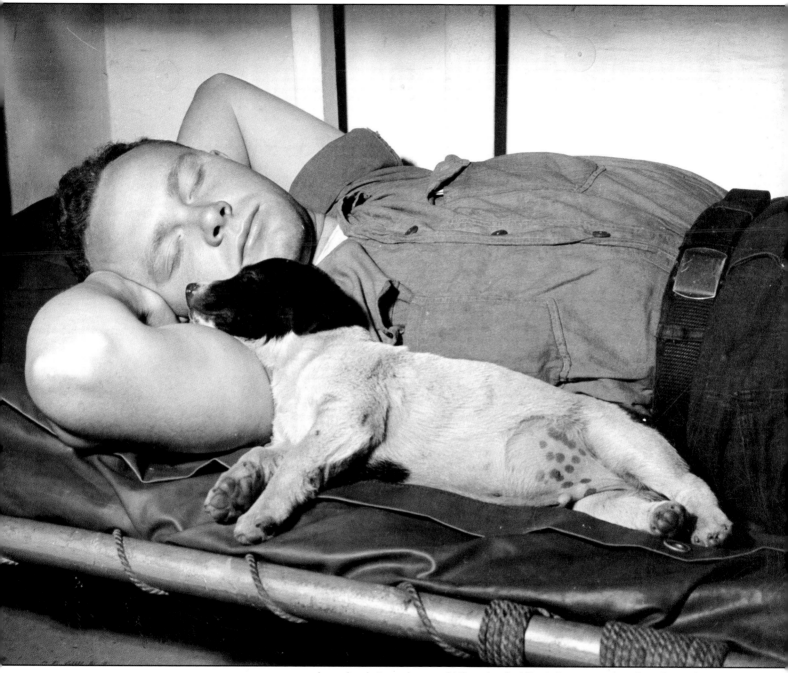

A sneaky photographer caught these two buddies trying to get some sleep. Guns, the mascot on this combat cutter, and his master hit the sack together after standing a long night's watch. They were in the waters off the French Mediterranean coast, where Operation Dragoon had just begun, landing 90,000 troops between Toulon and Cannes in August 1944.

When general quarters is sounded aboard this combat cutter, Sparky goes topside on the double. His battle station is flexible. He just goes where his fancy takes him.

Millions of American men are overseas fighting the enemy, but if any proof were needed that they're still pretty much the same kind of fellows who left home, this photo adds a convincing touch. Dogs and boys go together—and no matter where they are, when they can, boys take their pets along. These soldiers are part of a troop carrier force aboard a Coast Guard-manned troop transport in the Atlantic. They're being taken to an overseas base, where they will help ferry combat veterans home by air. You can be sure their dogs will travel with them.

Pete the Pooch, an able seaman, wasn't like other dogs. He was a mooring expert in the port at Le Havre, and he knew all about military ships and the different ways to moor them. He handled many vessels in his wartime life by jumping into the sea after the line, bringing it ashore, then making the vessel fast.

Hooligan has only one gripe against the life of a seafaring dog: the too-frequent bucket baths administered over his protests and sour expressions of indignation. Harry Scrutchfield, Kansas City, Missouri, does a job on Hooligan.

After a life of service to the guys at Hedron 12, Naval Air Station, Banana River, Florida, Skippy is honored with a full military funeral and burial. His remains are placed in an empty bomb casing, which will be dropped at sea.

Irish with his pals, somewhere in the Southwest Pacific.

For Irish, the fighting was about to begin. He had been the mongrel mascot of a Marine company in training back in the States, and when the boys were deployed overseas, they took him along. At the time the photo was taken, Irish was transferring with his company from a Coast Guard assault transport to an LST somewhere in the South Pacific. An assault against a Japanese-held island was about to begin. Tension on his leash indicated that Irish was eager to get down the gangway and get his paws on the beach.

CHAPTER 5

Semper Fido
Mascots of the U.S. Marine Corps

In the postwar years, the Marine Corps did a superb job organizing its World War II records. All of the photography was sorted and boxed according to the islands on which Marines fought. Iwo Jima, Tarawa, Guadalcanal, Eniwetok—each box of photos was subdivided by subject matter. Nevertheless, the classification system was sometimes confusing. For example, if an animal was in a particular snapshot, the photo was placed in a section aptly titled "Animals." Each box for each island had a section by that name.

Despite this rather direct, to-the-point classification system, it was disappointing to find that most of the Marine Corps animal photos did not show warm companions. Rather, the images recorded the Marines' disciplined, impersonal "war dogs." The Marines were prolific users of dogs as weapons. Used to sniff out Japanese caves, tunnels, and foxholes, these were not the men's mascots, but rather, a significant part of the Pacific war machine. But there were mascots a plenty: you just had to keep a keen eye out for what you were seeing. Instead of dogs, the photographs revealed that the mascots often were rather exotic pets like parrots, snakes, and even cats. In the Far Pacific, cats were found in abundance, much more so than dogs.

That said, the Marines had some wonderful dogs, and taken together, this collection is one of the most intriguing in this book. Without doubt, some of the most endearing mascot photography comes from these files. Parrots, roosters, donkeys, and dogs were all mascots that contrast beautifully with these hearty Marines.

A Marine aviation squadron poses with its mascot, Stinko, on Guadalcanal in 1943.

Marine Corporal Virgil Burgess in his foxhole with
Prince. Prince was one of several dogs used by the
Marines to run messages between the front lines and
the rear command post. Taken on Iwo Jima, 1945.

Fourth Division Marines headed for the shore on Iwo Jima shortly after H-hour in the invasion of this Pacific island. February 19, 1945.

Private PCI, pet of Marine Private Theodore Carter, is carrying out his own personal occupation of Japan. Carter brought his pup all the way from Hawaii and takes him ashore in the landing craft with the rest of the Marines.

Cheewa, a small spider monkey, is pals with the Marines on Okinawa. Here he hugs up against Private Elwood Smith.

War and Conflict, *an exhibit tracing the history of Americans at war developed by the researchers at the National Archives, included this powerful image of a weary Marine asleep in his foxhole guarded by his trusted companion.*

How about a goat? Corporal Gerard Ford with his goat mascot he picked up on Okinawa.

Right: Corporal Edward Burckhardt with kitten that he said "captured" him at the base of Suribachi on the battlefield of Iwo Jima.

Banzai, a monkey pal of hospital corpsman Robert Paul, is the official greeter at the medical offices on Okinawa.

Corporal John Rueschlin of Paterson, New Jersey, fondles a native kid after his return form the Saipan front lines for a rest, 1944.

Eight naval airmen and their dog, Turbo, were rescued by Coast Guard Air-Sea Rescue out of San Diego, California, after their plane crashed in the Pacific.

Andy, a Doberman pinscher and Private First Class Lansley of Syracuse, New York, of the Second Marine Raiders in Bougainville prepare to cross a road. War correspondents wrote instructions on this photo to crop it with an eye toward the triangulation between the eyes of the marine, his dog, and the gun.

It didn't take Killer long to catch on to what's what on Okinawa. Right after the first Japanese air raid, she followed the example of her Marine buddies and dug herself a foxhole.

These Waterbury, Connecticut, Marines are readying themselves for the next push. With them is Zombie, a five-foot snake mascot of their platoon.

With a steel helmet for a pillow and the coral ground for a bed, a Sixth Division Marine and a "friend" take a well-earned rest in front of a 105-millimeter howitzer on Okinawa. The tired artilleryman is John Emmons of Sheffield, Alabama. Friend is the unit mascot.

Private Chico, a two-month-old wire fox terrier, poses before the foxhole he dug immediately after landing on Bougainville. Private Chico was found wandering around on New Georgia by a Marine aviation ground crew.

Right: Finding refuge in war for some may have been found by adopting a dog, cat, or even a chicken. For others, refuge was a cool dip after a long, hard tank ride

Got a light, mate? Heckle, one of the pair of crows raised as pets by members of the 9th Marines, accepts a light from Sergeant Wayne Kelly of Grant, Kentucky. Heckle, along with his brother (or sister?) Jekyll, has picked up several such accomplishments from the Leathernecks.

A small Okinawa goat has adopted the Marines of the Headquarters Company, First Marine Division. Shown here up to her usual tricks, the goat seems to be getting into everyone's hair. Two Marines find themselves in a game of leapfrog with this self-imposed mascot.

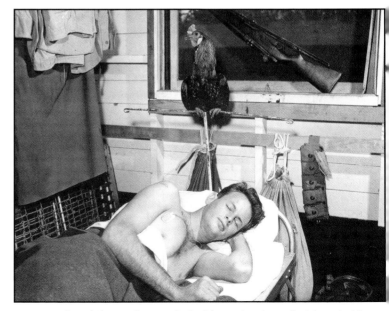

An aviation engineer waits for his rooster-alarm clock to wake him up.

Bowing from his perch high atop the cowling of a new F4U Corsair is Bilge, mascot of the Marines' "Flying Bulldogs" squadron stationed in Okinawa in 1945.

Buddy stands in sorrow at the grave of his master in the 5th Marine Division. Buddy has been at the front since the invasion of Iwo Jima.

CHAPTER 6

Jubilee
War's End

Mascot photography continued as the war came to an end—and why not? After endless days in wet foxholes and countless months living on ships that pitched to and fro, who better to share the joyous moment with than the one buddy who stood by your side through it all. This short section memorializes the final day of World War II and the subsequent process of packing up and going home. You'll see our boys turn flares into victory celebrations, sing songs on their bombs, and then, without fear of bullets flying through the air, begin the process of packing up and shipping out. Once again, mascots are right by their sides, some saying goodbye, some confused by it all, others being stuffed into a duffel bag for the long ride home. The war had ended, but not the bond. As we see in these photographs, soldier and mascot together looked forward to friends, family, a hot meal—and time to revel in the long-awaited peace.

War's end was an event shared by all, in this case sailor and mascot alike. Wrote the correspondent who captioned this photo: "Shouting wildly with joy, these happy sailors in the Navy Yard at Pearl Harbor register their reaction to the news of wars end."

Big Foot joins his mates in a little celebratory harmony. The soldiers are Flying Fortress ordnance men. Big Foot is known as a crooning canine.

Boys will be boys, and a case of flares is put to good use when news of Germany's surrender reaches them.

Sergeant Wallace Moore of Edenton, North Carolina, ties up his terrier, Tony, in his B barracks bag to make sure he isn't left behind. Sergeant Moore leaves nothing to chance and stencils Tony's bag carefully.

A number of joyous Second Division Marines about to board ship after 30 months overseas were not forgotten by the famed division mascot, Eightball, who was on hand to bid them a sorrowful good-bye.

Bringing up the rear for three Marines in the streets of Okinawa is their diminutive mascot.

Snafu, mascot of an engineer firefighting platoon in Belgium, waits at the station door for the men to return from an alarm.

CHAPTER 7

Who Said I'm a Dog?
Humor in the Face of War

Mascot photography was at times poignant, at other times inspiring, and often dramatic. But mascot photography was also humorous, too, and to those who say it is the nature of man to make war, these final photographs are for you. Despite the horrors around them, when there was any lull in the action, the pranks began. What better way to relieve the stress than to wrap a frilly dress around a dog, or pose a mascot just so? Taken together, humor was the right touch. It was the break from reality that soldiers needed.

How, though, to display these shots? Positioning sight gags next to a battle sequence trivializes war. How can one juxtapose a B-17 bomber under the withering gunfire of a German fighter attack with a dog dressed in a frilly hat? The answer is simple. One can't. Instead, some of the most amusing and some of the silliest mascot photography from World War II appears in this final section.

These last photos are included as a curtain call—a fitting end to this book. It was laughter, not war, that our boys wanted in 1941. Posed with their dogs, they revealed what a great generation they truly were. Now, so many years later, the portrait is nothing short of unique: World War II. Men. And dogs. Juxtaposed, the photos reveal a bond that melded the innocence of the time with the hardened necessity of a soldier. This bond was simple, timeless, and yet, indescribable. Photos could capture it, but no one could duplicate it. Though weapons proliferated, battles escalated, and legions of soldiers answered the call of their flag, no war power could destroy the sense of the loyalty, commitment, and devotion that exists only between a man and a dog.

Soogie.

Spar, wearing
dress blues before
going ashore.

Left to right—Utah, D-Day, Yappey, Muff, Red, Lightning, and Blackie. D-Day plus 4, off the coast of France.

Staff Sergeant Spike eating meat loaf during a party in his honor at the end of the war.

Right: Barnacle Bill, somewhere in the Pacific.

Talasea, a kitten pet, in the shirt of a homeward-bound Marine.

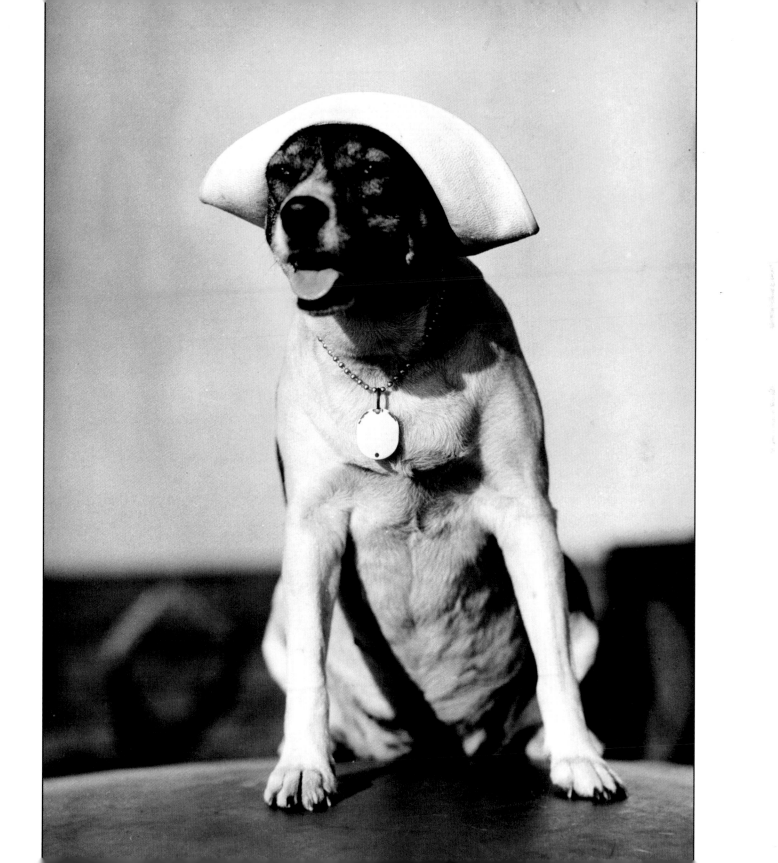

Even a dog has to cut loose. Scrappy is seen here at Pearl Harbor with a flash light in his mouth when he got the drift of the flash that the Japanese had accepted the Potsdam surrender terms.

It's humiliatin' that's what it is. Just plain humiliatin'. Here I make the
hop to England in a four-engine job, and they give me the moniker
Trans-Atlantic Topper, and now, just like that, I'm back to primary.

A Marine in the II Photo Division thought this pretty well summed up how it felt to be a combat photographer.

Oki, Nawa, and Shima are petted and spoiled by their Marines as much as a baby is spoiled by a doting grandmother.

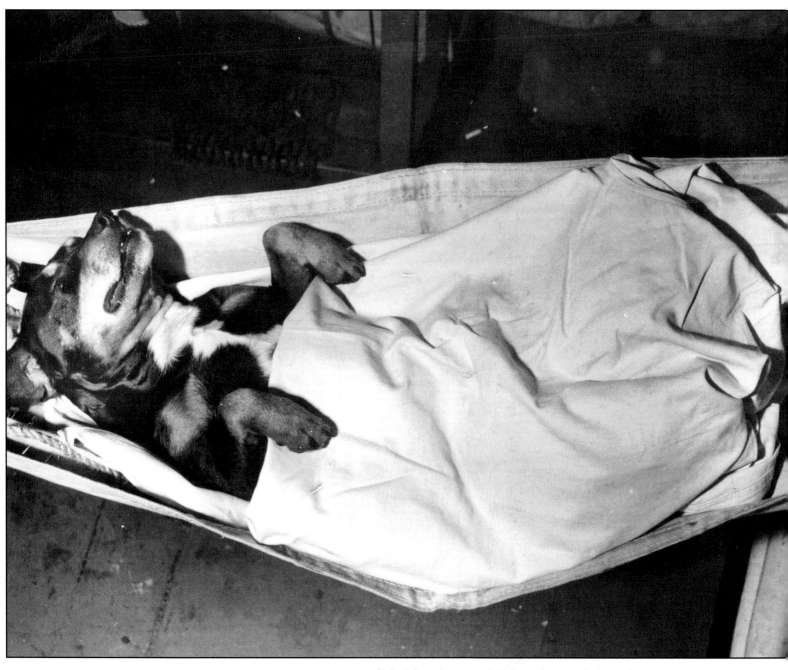

Sinbad, famed mascot of the Coast Guard, is in the doghouse again. After a big night of shore liberty with the boys, he failed muster and stayed sacked in, in his specially made sea hammock. Sinbad is a gay blade with the ladies and, surpassing his shipmates, has several in every port.

A gold-bricker, Hobo reluctantly stirs himself from the sack.

Mike poses again for a cameraman. (see page 29)

Bozo watches his pals go ashore. His sad expression convinced the skipper to allow Bozo to join them

Buddies.
In memory of the men
and women who fought
World War II—and the
four-legged companions
that stood by their side.

Index

Airplanes
   Honey Chile, 46
   Memphis Belle, 49
   Ole Miss, 31
   Our Gang, 40
   Up 'n Front, 47
   Skippy, 38
Birds, 82, 121, 134
   Heckle, 132
   Japo, 110
   Jekyll, 132
   Jockey, 63
Cats, 126
   Talasea, 146
Dogs
   Andy, 130
   Arab, 56
   Barnacle Bill, 105, 146
   Barney, 69
   Big Foot, 139
   Bilge, 135
   Blackie, 144
   Blackout, 87
   Blondie, 47
   Boots, 12, 31, 34, 80
   Bozo, 154
   Buddy, 27, 135
   Bullseye, 11
   Bunky, 101
   Cherbourg, 80
   Chippie, 23
   Cognac, 26
   D-Day, 144
   D-Day plus 4, 144
   Doc Sunshine, 96–98
   Dud, 21
   Fido, 75
   Flash, 61
   Fossill, 66
   Friend, 131
   General, 26
   Ginger, 23, 28
   Half Hitch, 96
   H.E. Kelly, 95
   Herbert, 43
   Hobo, 58, 152
   Hooligan, 116
   Invader, 108
   Irish, 119
   Jack, 101
   Jerry, 50
   Jo Ann, 83
   Joe, 110

Joe Kodachrome, 28
Jumper, 20
Junior, 19
Kelly, 10
Killer, 130
Knobby, 103
Leipzig, 29
Lightning, 144
Little Joe, 24
Max, 9, 15, 17
Midnight, 80
Mike, 29, 89, 153
Mr. Chips, 89
Muff, 144
Mutt, 99
Nawa, 150
Oki, 150
Pepper, 87
Pete the Pooch, 114
Petie, 12
Pistol, 55
Prince, 122
Private Chico, 132
Private PCI, 124
Red, 144
Queenie, 85
Rosie, 70
Rusty Robin, 109
Saki, 92
Salty, 15, 53, 90
Scrappy, 148
Shima, 150
Sinbad, 10, 77, 151
Skippy, 31, 38, 39, 117
Smokey, 73
Snafu, 141
Snuffy, 65
Soogie, 77, 143
Spar, 144
Sparky, 67, 92, 103, 106, 112
Spike, 146
Steamboat, 70
Stinko, 121
Stuka, 49
Texas Ranger, 34
Tony, 140
Tracer, 51
Trans-Atlantic Topper, 149
Trixie, 33
Turbo, 129
Utah, 144
Yappy, 144
Goats, 126, 129, 134

Monkeys, 41, 150
   Banzai, 126
   Cheewa, 124
   Eightball, 141
   Tojo, 13
People
   Adams, Harold, 90
   Barnes, Elmer, 80
   Benedict, Major Bill, 45
   Burgess, Virgil, 122
   Burkhardt, Cpl. Edward, 126
   Carter, Pvt. Theodore, 124
   David, Pfc. J.H., 23
   Dixon, Lt. Commander Jack, 94
   Emmons, John, 131
   Enos, Erwin, 87
   Ertzweiller, Henry, 23
   Fennell, Pvt. Jesse, 21
   Fontana, Pvt. Calvin J., 23, 28
   Ford, Cpl. Gerald, 126
   Gabriele, Cpl. Joseph, 22
   Gavin, Col. James M., 15
   Giangrasso, Boatswain's Mate
     Carmine, 75
   Goldenberger, Lt. Col., 46
   Greene, Sgt. Troy, 22
   Hancock, Pvt. Frank, 26
   Jackson, Lt. Stanley K., 75
   Keel, Pfc. Harold, 97
   Kelly, Sgt. Wayne, 132
   Kenworth, H.W., 59
   Landon, Brig. Gen. Truman, 43
   Lansley, Pfc., 130
   Leaf, Capt. Charles, 45
   Lynch, Edward, 87
   Mediroa, Tech. Spec., 4, 24
   Moore, Sgt. Wallace, 140
   Murray, Sgt. Peter, 26
   Paul, Robert, 126
   Patrick, Sgt. John, 33
   Post, Keinard, 78
   Ramsey, Ens. Clifford, 65
   Roosevelt, President Franklin D.
     12, 14
   Rueschlin, Cpl. John, 129
   Scatko, Cpl. Frederick, 26
   Scrutchfield, Harry, 116
   Sinkwich, Frank, 50
   Smith, Pvt. Elwood, 124
   Smith, Seaman 1st. Cl. Kenneth,
     92
   Stump, Lt. Russell, 35
   Snafu, Pvt., 7, 9

Travis, Brig. Gen. Robert, 42
Vespa, George, 20
Walker, Capt. Ralph, 27
Yakich, Ens. John, 61
Places
   Banana River, Florida, 117
   Bastogne, Belgium, 10
   Chalons, France, 27
   Fort Benning, Georgia, 7, 17
   Galvaston, Texas, 77
   Haiming, Austria, 28
   Harlingen, Texas, 51
   Honolulu, Hawaii, 78
   Iwo Jima, 10, 36, 121–123
   Kwajalein, Gilbert Islands, 43
   Le Havre, France, 19, 114
   Leipzig, Germany, 29
   London, England, 28
   Oberwessel, Germany, 25
   Pearl Harbor, Hawaii, 7, 53, 148
   Pelileu, 10
Ships
   Harris, 89
   LC 1947, 66
   Milletle, 54
   PCE 851, 65
   Wasp, 78
Units
   1st Marine Division, 134
   2nd Air Force, 50
   2nd Marine Raiders, 130
   4th Marine Division, 123, 141
   5th Army, 45
   5th Marine Division, 135
   6th Marine Division, 131
   7th Bomber Command, 43
   7th Fighter Command, 36, 44
   16th Fighter Squadron, 41
   16th Observation Squadron, 33
   26th Infantry Division, 24
   44th Infantry Division, 23
   44th Military Police Platoon, 28
   82nd Airborne Division, 19
   89th Infantry Division, 25
   95th Infantry Division, 23
   101st Airborne Division, 19, 21
   324th Bomb Squadron, 40
   337th Infantry Regiment, 21
   379th Bomb Group, 42
   452nd Bomb Group, 47
   505th Parachute Infantry Regimen[t]
   766th Light Ordnance Company,